OCTOBER 2016

Perspectives on Security and Strategic Stability

A Track 2 Dialogue with the Baltic States and Poland

PROJECT DIRECTORS
Kathleen H. Hicks
Heather A. Conley

AUTHORS
Lisa Sawyer Samp
Jeffrey Rathke
Anthony Bell

A REPORT OF THE
CSIS INTERNATIONAL SECURITY AND EUROPE PROGRAMS

CSIS | CENTER FOR STRATEGIC &
INTERNATIONAL STUDIES

ROWMAN & LITTLEFIELD
Lanham • Boulder • New York • London

About CSIS

For over 50 years, the Center for Strategic and International Studies (CSIS) has worked to develop solutions to the world's greatest policy challenges. Today, CSIS scholars are providing strategic insights and bipartisan policy solutions to help decisionmakers chart a course toward a better world.

CSIS is a nonprofit organization headquartered in Washington, DC. The Center's 220 full-time staff and large network of affiliated scholars conduct research and analysis and develop policy initiatives that look into the future and anticipate change.

Founded at the height of the Cold War by David M. Abshire and Admiral Arleigh Burke, CSIS was dedicated to finding ways to sustain American prominence and prosperity as a force for good in the world. Since 1962, CSIS has become one of the world's preeminent international institutions focused on defense and security; regional stability; and transnational challenges ranging from energy and climate to global health and economic integration.

Thomas J. Pritzker was named chairman of the CSIS Board of Trustees in November 2015. Former U.S. deputy secretary of defense John J. Hamre has served as the Center's president and chief executive officer since 2000.

CSIS does not take specific policy positions; accordingly, all views expressed herein should be understood to be solely those of the author(s).

ISBN: 978-1-4422-7960-5 (pb); 978-1-4422-7961-2 (eBook)

Center for Strategic & International Studies
1616 Rhode Island Avenue, NW
Washington, DC 20036
202-887-0200 | www.csis.org

Rowman & Littlefield
4501 Forbes Boulevard
Lanham, MD 20706
301-459-3366 | www.rowman.com

Contents

Acknowledgments

This project would not have been possible without the combined efforts of the International Security Program and the Europe Program at CSIS. The project directors and the authors would like to thank the many experts and staff throughout CSIS who contributed to the study, including Max Shafron, Rebecca Hersman, Olga Oliker, Adam Saxton, Kathleen Weinberger, Grant Murphy, and John O'Grady.

The study team is also grateful to the numerous experts in Lithuania, Latvia, Estonia, Poland, and the United States for sharing their time and insights at various points throughout the study process. In particular, the CSIS team thanks the Latvian Institute of International Affairs (LIIA), the International Centre for Defence and Security (ICDS, Estonia), and the Polish Institute of International Affairs (PISM) for helping facilitate a series of productive working groups in the Baltic States and Poland. This study has been dramatically improved by insights shared in the countries mentioned, as well as in the United States.

Finally, the study team thanks the Defense Threat Reduction Agency's Project on Advanced Systems and Concepts for Counter WMD (PASCC) at the Naval Postgraduate School, which sponsored this work and saw the value in growing a dialogue with Polish and Baltic civil society regarding the threats facing the North Atlantic Treaty Organization (NATO) to the east and the consequences for the United States and NATO. The team is deeply appreciative of PASCC's respect for our intellectual independence at each step along the way. The content and recommendations presented—including any errors—remain solely those of the authors.

Introduction

The Baltic States and Poland have been the primary focus of NATO's assurance and deterrence efforts since Russia's invasion of Ukraine in 2014. In the wake of the crisis, U.S. and allied officials adopted a policy approach that was heavily influenced by the perceptions and requests for assistance coming from their Eastern European counterparts. Vice President Joe Biden flew to Poland and Lithuania in March 2014 (just as President Vladimir Putin was annexing Crimea) to meet with the president and prime minister of Poland and the presidents of Estonia, Latvia, and Lithuania. He assured them that the United States understood their fears and that its commitment to "mutual self-defense under Article 5 of NATO remains ironclad."[1] President Barack Obama traveled to Estonia in September 2014, ahead of the NATO Summit in Wales, to do the same. U.S. national security officials at virtually every level have taken comparable trips, sought similar engagements, and received impressively consistent messages from their Baltic and Polish equivalents up and down the chain of command. These messages typically include condemnation of Russia's actions in Ukraine; emphasis of the threat that President Putin poses to all of NATO; and requests for more allied contingency planning and greater military presence in NATO's east to bolster deterrence and demonstrate alliance strength, resolve, and unity.

As NATO and the United States seek to expand their presence along the alliance's eastern flank, including with the deployment of four NATO battalions to the region and a U.S. infusion of $3.4 billion in 2017, it becomes increasingly important to engage representatives of civil society (nongovernment or "Track 2" interlocutors) in the Baltic States and Poland to better understand whether assurance efforts are having the desired effect and whether the statements and requests of the Baltic and Polish governments are, by and large, consistent with the attitudes and desires of

---

1. Joe Biden, "Remarks to the Press by Vice President Joe Biden with President Bronislaw Komorowski of Poland," White House, Office of the Vice President (Presidential Palace, Warsaw, Poland, March 18, 2014), https://www .whitehouse.gov/the-press-office/2014/03/18/remarks-press-vice-president-joe-biden-president-bronislaw -komorowski-po.

their local populations.[2] To that end, the Center for Strategic and International Studies (CSIS) executed a dialogue with local civil society leaders, security experts and academics, and government representatives from across the Baltic States, Poland, and the United States. The end result is a richer understanding among all parties regarding the shared threats and challenges facing Europe's eastern flank; the perceived effectiveness of the overall response from NATO, including the United States, in addressing them; and the implications for broader strategic stability.

SCOPE AND OBJECTIVES

This report presents the CSIS study team's key observations divided across five lines of inquiry: (1) regional perspectives on threats and vulnerabilities; (2) views on the U.S. and NATO roles in conventional deterrence in Eastern Europe; (3) regional approaches to internal defense and security; (4) the nuclear dimension on the eastern flank; and (5) future challenges to transatlantic cohesion. The objective of this project was to enhance scholarship on the enduring challenges stemming from the Ukraine crisis and to enhance public discussion of the evolving nature and future of security and defense relations between the United States, the Baltic States, and Poland.

The project was conducted between late 2015 and mid-2016. In addition to reviewing the academic literature coming out of the region, the study team traveled to Poland, Latvia, Lithuania, and Estonia in March 2016 to meet with regional security experts, academics, civil society leaders, journalists, government officials, independent researchers and bloggers, and regional U.S. government and military representatives. In addition to individual meetings and roundtables, workshops were convened in each country to bring the various representatives together and allow for an exchange of ideas. We also convened a two-day workshop in Washington, DC in May 2016 that brought together representatives from Europe- and U.S.-based research institutes, universities, and think tanks, as well as former and current U.S. government officials.

We view this report as one contribution to a larger and ongoing conversation and by no means an exhaustive review of the opinions held by citizens of the Baltic States and Poland. Further, all of the conversations conducted under the auspices of this project were under the Chatham House Rule. Any quotations attributed are drawn from published works, not from interviews we conducted. While the study team endeavored to honestly and accurately capture the perspectives of those that participated in our study, we recognize that personal filters inevitably create bias in reporting on the views and opinions of others. Any inaccuracies in capturing the views presented are our own.

---

2. NATO, "Warsaw Summit Communiqué," press release, July 9, 2016, http://www.nato.int/cps/en/natohq/official_texts_133169.htm; White House, "Fact Sheet: The FY2017 European Reassurance Initiative Budget Request," February 2, 2016, https://www.whitehouse.gov/the-press-office/2016/02/02/fact-sheet-fy2017-european-reassurance-initiative-budget-request.

Brief History of Relations with Russia

An historical accounting of the complicated relationships between Russia, the Baltics States, and Poland is beyond the scope of this report. That said, it is impossible to understand the perspectives of the Polish and Baltic populations without first being aware of a few key events from the past that continue to shape relations today.

BALTIC STATES

While there are a number of factors that differentiate each of the three Baltic States, the region as a whole shares a deep and intertwined history with Russia. Latvia, Lithuania, and Estonia—incorporated into the Russian Empire in the 18th century—gained their independence at the tumultuous conclusion of World War I and the Russian Revolution. The Baltic States emerged as modern nation-states in the early 1920s, but their independence was short-lived. All three states were invaded and annexed by the Soviet Union in 1940, occupied by Nazi Germany from 1941 to 1944, and then reoccupied by the Soviets toward the end of World War II. The Soviet annexation of the Baltic States was never recognized as legitimate by the United States and many European powers. Over the following decades, the Baltic States experienced the shared trauma of mass exiles, forced collectivization, linguistic-cultural Russification, and attempts to extinguish their national identities.

The Baltic States also share a similar liberation experience. Anti-Soviet protest movements began in all three states in 1988, and in 1989 the citizens of Estonia, Latvia, and Lithuania staged a human "Baltic Chain" across the region as a nonviolent demonstration against Soviet rule. As the Soviet system weakened, Lithuania was the first Soviet republic to declare independence in 1990, quickly followed by Estonia and Latvia. Moscow undertook a violent crackdown in Lithuania and Latvia in January 1991. The collapsing Soviet Union was unable to halt the momentum of Baltic independence, and after the failed coup attempt in the Soviet Union in August 1991, the three countries' independence was recognized by Western countries as well as the Soviet Union.

Following independence, the Baltic States followed a pro-Western path that culminated in all three countries joining the European Union (EU) and NATO in 2004. The political situation in the Baltic States and their relationships with Russia are complicated by the fact that all three countries contain ethnic Russian minority populations. According to demographic data collected in 2011, ethnic Russians account for 25 percent of the population in Estonia, 26 percent in Latvia, and 6 percent in Lithuania.[1] Prior to the Soviet annexation, all of the Baltic States had relatively small Russian populations. Upon annexation, Soviet authorities encouraged Russians to move to the Baltics ostensibly to support industrialization efforts, though some regional historians view the policy as a way to "exterminate all obvious manifestations of ethnic historical survival."[2] Lithuania was not as greatly populated with ethnic Russians during the Soviet period because the demand for industrial workers was already greatly filled by the native Lithuanian population, and to this day Lithuania has a significantly smaller percentage of Russians than its Baltic neighbors.[3] The presence of these populations has been used by Russia as pretext for involvement in the Baltic region; Russian troops remained in Lithuania until 1993 and in Estonia and Latvia until 1994 allegedly, in part, to guarantee the security of the states' ethnic Russians postindependence.[4]

The political weight of ethnic Russian minorities is arguably the most pronounced in Latvia. In recent years, the country has seen increased support for the center-left Harmony party, which has traditionally drawn its support from Latvia's ethnically Russian citizens. Russian support for the Harmony party has been described by opponents as pushing for a "little green president."[5] In 2014, the party received more votes than any other single party in the parliamentary elections, winning 24 of 100 parliamentary seats; however, no other party was willing to join it in a coalition given its ties to Putin's United Russia party.[6] That Harmony was able to garner such a large percentage of the vote despite almost 30 percent of the ethnic Russian population remaining disenfranchised—due to either a personal choice to remain a "noncitizen" or the restrictive Latvian language and history tests needed to become a citizen—is noteworthy.[7]

---

1. "Estonia," "Latvia," and "Lithuania," *The World Factbook* (Washington, DC: Central Intelligence Agency, 2011), https://www.cia.gov/library/publications/the-world-factbook/.

2. Dina Zisserman-Brodsky, *Construction Ethnopolitics in the Soviet Union: Samizdat, Deprivation, and the Rise of Ethnic Nationalism* (London: Palgrave Macmillan, 2003), 94; Andrejs Plankans, *A Concise History of the Baltic States* (Cambridge: Cambridge University Press, 2011); Marina Best, "The Ethnic Russian Minority: A Problematic Issue in the Baltic States," *Verges: Germanic & Slavic Studies in Review* 2, no. 1 (2013): 33–41.

3. Plankans, *A Concise History of the Baltic States*; Best, "The Ethnic Russian Minority"; Aldis Purs, *Baltic Facades* (London: Reaktion Books, 2012).

4. Rita P. Peters, "Russia, the Baltic States and the West," *Demokratizatsiya: The Journal of Post-Soviet Democratization* 2, no. 4 (Fall 1994): 623–624.

5. Janis Kazocins, "Will Latvia Be Putin's Next Victim?," in *Latvian Foreign and Security Policy: Yearbook 2015*, ed. Andris Sprūds and Diāna Potjomkina (Riga: Latvian Institute of International Affairs, 2015), 71–78.

6. "How to Deal with Harmony," *Economist*, October 6, 2014, http://www.economist.com/blogs/easternapproaches/2014/10/latvias-election.

7. David Klion, "Latvian Election Results Underscore Regional Tensions with Russia," *World Politics Review*, October 10, 2014, http://www.worldpoliticsreview.com/trend-lines/14184/latvian-election-results-underscore-regional-tensions-with-russia.

Estonia has also experienced ethnic frictions in recent years. In 2007, an effort by the Estonian government to relocate a Soviet-era memorial dedicated to Red Army soldiers in World War II—which some ethnic Estonians believed symbolized the Soviet occupation—triggered violent protests by ethnic Russians in Tallinn.[8] Estonia's ethnic Russian community opposed the relocation, viewing the memorial as a symbol of the sacrifices made during the Soviet victory over Nazi Germany and the move as an affront to their rights within Estonian society. The relocation of the memorial was strongly criticized by the Kremlin and the Russian Duma voted for sanctions to be imposed on Estonia.[9] The protests in Tallinn, which became known as Bronze Night, were coupled with a series of crippling cyberattacks believed to have originated in Russia.[10]

The Baltic States have more recently found themselves the target of Russian airspace violations, threatening statements, and numerous military exercises (sometimes conducted without any advance notice) in proximity to their borders, such as a March 2015 snap exercise that brought 80,000 Russian troops to full combat readiness.[11] In addition, the Baltics were warned that if they chose to take part in NATO plans for missile defense systems, they would be considered "targets" by Russia's military.[12]

POLAND

Throughout the Cold War, communist Poland experienced waves of political and social unrest aimed at the oppressive policies of the Soviet-backed regime. The Polish people regularly took to the streets to protest communist leadership, beginning with the Poznań Uprising of 1956 and culminating with the Solidarity movement that began in 1980 and stretched across the decade.[13] Government security forces were frequently called on to put down the protests, often leading to violent clashes.[14] The protests and the bloody reprisals they elicited from the Soviet-backed authorities are memorialized throughout Poland today and remain fresh in the minds of the Polish people.

Since the collapse of Poland's communist regime in 1989 and the fall of the Soviet Union, Polish relations with Russia can be characterized as generally negative. A 2015 Pew Research poll shows

8. "Tallinn Tense after Deadly Riots," *BBC News*, April 28, 2007, http://news.bbc.co.uk/2/hi/europe/6602171.stm.

9. Steven Lee Myers, "Estonia Removes Soviet-era War Memorial after a Night of Violence," *New York Times*, April 27, 2007, http://www.nytimes.com/2007/04/27/world/europe/27iht-estonia.4.5477141.html.

10. See Stephen Herzog, "Revisiting the Estonian Cyber Attacks: Digital Threats and Multinational Responses," in "Strategic Security in the Cyber Age," special issue, *Journal of Strategic Studies* 4, no. 2 (Summer 2011): 49–60.

11. Agence France-Presse, "Russia Expands Military Exercises to 80,000 Troops," Defense News, March 19, 2015, http://www.defensenews.com/story/defense/international/europe/2015/03/19/russia-expands-military-exercises-troops/25023979/.

12. Thomas Barrabi, "Russia Warns Baltic States NATO's Anti-Missile Shield Will Make Them 'Targets,'" *International Business Times*, June 24, 2015, http://www.ibtimes.com/russia-warns-baltic-states-natos-anti-missile-shield-will-make-them-targets-1981588.

13. David Ost, *The Defeat of Solidarity: Anger and Politics in Postcommunist Europe* (Ithaca, NY: Cornell University Press, 2005).

14. Abraham Brumberg, "Poland: The Demise of Communism," *Foreign Affairs* 69 (1990): 71–82.

80 percent of Poles having an "unfavorable" view of Russia.[15] There have been attempts at relationship building between the two governments, but these efforts hit a major stumbling block in 2010, when 95 senior Polish political and military officials, including President Lech Kaczyński, were killed in a plane crash near Smolensk, Russia. The crash occurred while the delegation was en route to Russia to commemorate the Katyn massacre—the execution of 22,000 Polish elites, including much of the Polish officer corps, by Soviet secret police in 1940, and another source of national resentment toward Russia. One-third of Poles believe that the crash may have been an assassination, beliefs occasionally stoked by Polish politicians from the governing Law and Justice Party. Poland's Foreign Minister Witold Waszczykowski said he "cannot rule out the possibility" of malicious intent.[16] While separate Russian and Polish investigations have pointed to pilot error and poor weather, the Smolensk crash continues to cast a shadow over Poland's relationship with Russia.

One of the most contentious topics in Polish-Russian relations is the impending presence of a U.S. missile defense site in Redzikowo, a small Polish village situated on the Baltic Sea and not far from the Russian enclave of Kaliningrad.[17] Russian officials assert that the system undermines its strategic deterrent and have labeled Poland and Romania (another host to components of NATO's missile defense architecture) as "objects of priority response," meaning they will be targeted early in the event of a conflict with NATO.[18] In 2009 and 2014, Russian exercises simulated attacks on Poland from Kaliningrad.

15. Bruce Stokes, "Russia, Putin Held in Low Regard around the World," Pew Research Center, August 5, 2015, http://www.pewglobal.org/2015/08/05/russia-putin-held-in-low-regard-around-the-world/.

16. Wiktor Szary, "Polish Refocus on Smolensk Crash Could Hurt Relations with Russia," Reuters, November 26, 2016, http://www.reuters.com/article/us-poland-smolensk-idUSKBN0TF0ON20151126.

17. Lisa Ferdinando, "Work Joins Groundbreaking for Ballistic Missile Defense Site in Poland," U.S. Department of Defense, May 13, 2015, http://www.defense.gov/News/Article/Article/759662/work-joins-groundbreaking-for-ballistic-missile-defense-site-in-poland.

18. Paul Sonne, "Russia Threatens NATO over Missile Shield," *Wall Street Journal*, April 16, 2015, http://www.wsj.com/articles/russia-threatens-nato-over-missile-shield-1429185058.

02

Regional Perspectives on Threats and Vulnerabilities

Our research affirmed the existence of broad consensus among the Baltic States and Poland on the nature of their security threats at a macro-level of analysis. An overwhelming majority agreed that Russia is by far the most concerning external (and existential) threat facing the region. Other external pressures, such as terrorism or migration, were generally only cited as a threat insofar as they could potentially distract allies from focusing on the "real" threat—Russia. While the interlocutors we spoke with tended to agree that the fear of imminent Russian aggression—which prevailed at the start of the Ukraine crisis—had largely subsided, they assessed that it has been replaced by a persistent anxiety and an overall sense of resignation to the need to (re)adapt to life under the constant threat of Russian aggression. Despite near total agreement on the source of the threat, however, we uncovered a high degree of variation throughout the course of our research between and within these nations regarding the precise societal vulnerabilities magnifying it. The anxiety over Russia is compounded by the region's insecurities over U.S. and Western allies' level of commitment to collective defense.

There are three areas, in particular, that resident regional experts and members of civil society tended to highlight when discussing Russia-specific vulnerabilities in their nations and the region: (1) ethno-cultural sympathies, including the susceptibility to a Ukraine-like "little green men" scenario and the receptivity of the local population to propaganda; (2) cyber weaknesses; and (3) conventional military imbalance (nuclear concerns are discussed separately in Section 5). With the exception of the conventional military category, which we consistently found to be the most concerning to those we spoke with by a large margin, there were widely different perspectives on the vulnerability each nation faces from Russia. Our research revealed that the high degree of awareness and unease surrounding Moscow's conventional military advantage was in large part due to Russia's proximity to NATO's eastern flank and its ability to rapidly reposition a significant number of forces. The prospect of Russia directing its conventional military force at any one of the eastern flank nations dwarfed other concerns, including those related to lower-intensity hybrid warfare (e.g., "little green men") or those affecting Europe more broadly (e.g., terrorism).

ETHNO-CULTURAL SYMPATHIES

Sharp contrasts were uncovered regarding local perceptions of societal divisions and vulnerabilities related to the local Russian-speaking population's degree of disaffection and their susceptibility to Russian propaganda and coercion. Opinions varied most starkly in Latvia and Estonia, both of which, as previously mentioned, contain a large number of ethnic Russians and Russian-speakers. For those who perceive little to no ethno-cultural vulnerabilities, Russia's attempts to disseminate propagandistic information were described as futile since they believe Russian sources are not taken seriously outside of Russian circles.[1] According to these arguments, Russia simply does not have the same economic or informational leverage in the Baltic States, and certainly not in Poland, as it did in Ukraine. The Russian-speaking minorities in the Baltics are more dispersed than in Ukraine, although there are pockets of Russian-speaking populations near the border with Russia in northeastern Estonia and in southeastern Latvia. There are also no indigenous secessionist movements among the Baltic States' Russian-speaking minorities, which makes targeting and sustaining popular disaffection more difficult.

Estonian author Henrik Praks further argues that, in the Estonian case, ethnic Russian minorities have strong economic imperatives to remain within the EU member state and are therefore less likely to want to "change their status and become subjects of the Russian Federation."[2] Several Estonian observers we spoke with agreed and presented the view that it was extremely unlikely, some thought unimaginable, that Moscow's so-called hybrid warfare tactics could be successfully used against their country in fomenting an insurrection. In the event of a Ukraine-style land grab using "little green men," the group suggested that security forces would immediately resist and open fire, making such an attempt too high a risk from Moscow's perspective. This prediction of the state's response was attributed in part to Estonia having learned the lessons of history: Finland fought the Soviets in 1939 and stayed free; Estonia did not and was occupied for over 50 years. When queried about the effectiveness of Russian information operations, one former Estonian official offered that Estonians—including Russian-speakers—were "immune" to Russian propaganda and countered that the United States and Western Europe were far more vulnerable to Russian deception, especially with "RT in every hotel room."

Others were less sanguine and remain concerned that the political cleavages within Estonia and Latvia create opportunities for Russian information operations to stir unrest. Among this group, the risk of Russian manipulation was considered to be greatly increased by virtue of the large number of people who watch Russian TV channels, read Russian newspapers, and follow other mass media outlets that use Russian sources for information. Additionally, they argue, Moscow would only need to mobilize a small number—"several dozen to several hundred individuals"—of Russia sympathizers to foment a crisis with the potential to overwhelm the police and military forces and upend the country's politics. After all, they add, there were no secessionist movements in eastern

---

1. James Corum, *The Security Concerns of the Baltic States as NATO Allies* (Carlisle, PA: Strategic Studies Institute and U.S. Army War College Press, 2013).

2. Henrik Praks, "Hybrid or Not: Deterring and Defeating Russia's Ways of Warfare in the Baltics—the case of Estonia," NATO Defense College Research Paper 124, December 2015, http://www.ndc.nato.int/news/news.php?icode=887.

Ukraine before 2014, but one was manufactured fairly easily by co-opting a handful of people. For those on this side of the argument, a similar scenario is not inconceivable in the Baltics.

Latvian authors Andris Kudors and Gatis Pelnens emphasize the ability of Russian propaganda to cause ethnic Russians in Latvia to "become negatively disposed against the state of Latvia and the basic ideas forming it," and underline the threat posed by the potential of a separatist movement in the Latgale region bordering Russia.[3] Likewise, Estonian political scientist Juhan Kivirähk identifies the presence of ethnic Russians in Estonia as a "strategic vulnerability," stating that there are "two Estonias [which] do not fully trust each other."[4] Some interlocutors were critical of those Latvians and Estonians who dismiss the ethnic challenge, saying they are "deceiving themselves" in terms of the extent to which the Russian-speaking populations in each nation are fully integrated. One interlocutor in Tallinn noted that Estonia's Russian-speaking population is, in fact, skeptical toward both NATO and the United States, and that Russian social media networks and Kremlin-controlled information outlets were widespread and effective. But even those we spoke with who empha-sized the ethno-cultural challenge agreed that, while they can envision aggression from Moscow starting off with unconventional tactics, such propaganda dissemination or fomenting of unrest, any disturbance would quickly be followed up with a conventional invasion.

Our interlocutors in Poland and Lithuania, by contrast, were largely in agreement that Russian propaganda had little to no audience in their own countries due to the lack of a sizeable Russian minority that could be exploited by Moscow. They therefore felt less at risk of subversive infiltration by "little green men" able to prey on the grievances of locals. This is not to suggest that our Polish and Lithuanian participants did not perceive a Russia propaganda problem or doubt its ability to cause instability—one Polish interlocutor referred to Russia's New Generation Warfare strategy more broadly as a "nightmare, death-by-a-thousand-cuts scenario"—but simply that they saw themselves as perhaps less vulnerable than other nations that are starting off with a more sympa-thetic audience. In fact, Polish and Lithuanian counterparts in the region made the point that Latvia and Estonia should be much more worried about such a scenario than they seem to be, with one Polish representative stating, "It is perfectly realistic for part of Latvia to become a frozen conflict, which would end NATO." Beyond emphasizing the risk to Latvia, his comment alludes to a surprisingly prevalent distrust of NATO ever reaching consensus on an Article 5 response in the event of a Russian attack on allied territory in the east. In general, the Poles we met with seemed to be the most skeptical as to whether NATO could be counted on to come to their rescue; this dynamic will be discussed more in Section 3.

Regardless of disagreements over locals' susceptibility to Russian influence, no one we spoke with denied that Russia was waging an active and aggressive information and propaganda campaign directed at all populations, regardless of ethnic background, throughout the eastern flank, and especially in the Baltic States. Lithuanian authors Linas Kojala and Aivaras Zukauskas note, for

3. See Andris Kudors and Gatis Pelnens, "Diverging Faces of 'Soft Power' in Latvia between the EU and Russia," in *The Different Faces of 'Soft Power': The Baltic States and Eastern Neighborhood between Russia and the EU*, ed. Toms Rostoks and Andris Sprūds (Riga: Latvian Institute of International Affairs, 2015).

4. Juhan Kivirähk, "Integrating Estonia's Russian-Speaking Population: Findings of National Defense Opinion Surveys," ICDS Analysis, December 2014, http://www.icds.ee/fileadmin/media/icds.ee/failid/Juhan_Kivirahk_-_Integrating _Estonias_Russian-Speaking_Population.pdf.

example, that while Lithuania does not have a significant problem with official pro-Russia movements and that in general the population feels integrated into European politics and values, there is still a concerted Russian effort to destabilize Lithuania via informational, political, ethnic, and economic channels.[5] In carrying out its campaign, Russia relies heavily on two interrelated ideas: the first is that the Soviet annexation of the Baltic States in 1940 saved these countries from the Nazi fascist threat; the second attempts to build on the image of Russian/Soviet forces as antifascist by stating that modern Baltic governments themselves have fascist tendencies, which are borne out in their treatment of ethnic Russian minorities living there.

These ideas are also used to justify Russia's Compatriots Policy, which applies to "individuals who live outside of the borders of the Russian Federation itself yet feel they have a historical, cultural, and linguistic linkage with Russia."[6] The Compatriots Policy stipulates that Russia has the right to militarily intervene on humanitarian grounds in order to protect these individuals, millions of whom reside in former Soviet republics. According to much of the academic literature produced in the region, Russia's use of propaganda to discredit the Baltic States as neofascist is directly connected to the potential invocation of the Compatriots Policy as a pretext for annexing territory, as was done in Crimea, or engaging in armed conflict.[7] The Latvian Constitution Protection Bureau report of 2012 states:

> The hidden objective of Russia's foreign policy is to discredit Latvia worldwide by: reproaching Latvia for the rebirth of fascism and rewriting history, attributing to Latvia the image of a failed state, and emphasizing discrimination against the Russian-speaking population. [This] is the dominant national security risk for Latvia created by the Compatriots Policy.[8]

This messaging also allows Russia to strengthen support for interventionist policies with its own domestic population, building on the concept of a patriotic and ideologically pure "Ruskii Mir" (Russian World) in contrast with a morally corrupt Europe from which vulnerable populations must be saved.[9] For those that cite a significant concern related to the vulnerability of minority populations, these policies are the source of much consternation.

---

5. See Linas Kojala, Aivaras Zukauskas, and Ilvija Brūģe, "Russia's Soft Power in Lithuania: The Impact of Conflict in Ukraine," in *Latvian Foreign and Security Policy: Yearbook 2016*, ed. Andris Sprūds and Ilvija Brūģe (Riga: Latvian Institute of International Affairs, 2016).

6. Igor Zevelev, "The Russian World in Moscow's Strategy," Center for Strategic and International Studies, August 22, 2016, https://www.csis.org/analysis/russian-world-moscows-strategy.

7. See Nerijus Maliukevicius, "The Roots of Putin's Media Offensive in the Baltic States: Learning Lessons in Counterstrategies," in *Baltic Visions: European Cooperation Regional Stability*, ed. Kinga Redlowska (Warsaw: Foundation Institute for Eastern Studies, 2015), 32–43; Mike Winnerstig ed., *Tools of Destabilization: Russian Soft Power and Non-Military Influence in the Baltic States* (Stockholm: Swedish Defense Research Agency [FOI] Project on Security in the Neighborhood, 2014), http://www.foi.se/report?rNo=FOI-R--3990--SE; Kudors and Pelnens, "Diverging Faces of 'Soft Power' in Latvia."

8. Andris Kudors, "Russian Soft Power and Non-Military Influence: The View from Latvia," in Winnerstig, *Tools of Destabilization*, 81.

9. Andris Kudors, "'Russian World'—Russia's Soft Power Approach to Compatriots Policy," *Russian Analytical Digest* 81 (June 2010); Victoria Panova, "Russia's 'Soft' Policy Towards the Baltic States," in Sprūds and Brūģe, *Latvian Foreign and Security Policy: Yearbook 2016*.

CYBER WEAKNESS

The CSIS study team found a high degree of focus on the Russian cyber challenge across the Baltic States and Poland. Russian cyber warfare tactics cover a wide area, from distributing malware to infiltrating the operations of foreign governments to targeting users with psychological attacks based on misinformation meant to cause emotional trauma.[10] The Baltic region and its neighbors have already experienced a number of such cyberattacks. The largest was a series of distributed denial of service (DDoS) attacks on Estonia in 2007 amid the Bronze Night dispute. The attack effectively cut off access to Estonian government, banking, and media websites. Estonian counterparts described the attack as a watershed moment for the government that finally "set off the alarm bells" on the need to get serious about cyber vulnerabilities. Russia is also suspected to have carried out cyberattacks against key other institutions in the region, including the Norwegian energy sector (2011), the Danish and Finnish governments (2012 and 2013), and the Polish flagship airline, grounding flights at Warsaw's busiest airport and impacting hundreds of travelers (2015).[11]

One of the greatest cyber threats facing the Baltic States from Russia is in the form of advanced persistent threats (APTs). These attacks do not target individuals with the same goals as routine malware, which generally aim to steal a user's banking or identification information, but instead aim to infiltrate networks and collect strategically significant information for espionage purposes. These cyberattack campaigns—code-named Snake, Turla, Uroburos, the Dukes, and Pawn Storm, to name a few—specifically targeted government networks with the goal of creating Trojan backdoors to allow access into networks and transmit data back to the distributors.[12]

As a result of these attacks and their increasing severity and frequency, Baltic and Nordic countries, as well as Germany and Poland, have worked with NATO to conduct training exercises, such as Baltic Cyber Shield in 2010 and annual Locked Shields exercises since 2012. The Baltic States also cooperate with their Nordic neighbors in the pan-Nordic Cyber Warfare Collaboration Project (CWCP).[13] Estonia is host to the NATO Cooperative Cyber Defense Center of Excellence and has cultivated a national proficiency in preparing for and countering cyberattacks, particularly following its experience with the 2007 DDoS cyberattack. Additionally, at the Wales Summit in 2014, allied leaders declared that a cyberattack could reach the threshold of being considered an Article 5 attack and, at the Warsaw Summit in 2016, pledged to "strengthen and enhance the cyber defences of national networks and infrastructures, as a matter of priority."[14]

While the alliance has taken steps *qua* the alliance to protect NATO's secure communications network, national systems (including portions NATO may need to rely on in the event of a

---

10. Eve Hunter and Piret Pernik, "The Challenges of Hybrid Warfare," ICDS Analysis, April 2015, http://www.icds.ee /fileadmin/media/icds.ee/failid/Eve_Hunter__Piret_Pernik_-_Challenges_of_Hybrid_Warfare.pdf.

11. Piret Pernik and Patrik Maldre, "Rising Challenges: Cybersecurity in the Baltic Sea Region," in Redlowska, *Baltic Visions*, 44–52.

12. See Patrik Maldre, "Global Connections, Regional Implications: An Overview of the Baltic Cyber Threat Landscape," ICDS Analysis, October 2015, http://www.icds.ee/fileadmin/media/icds.ee/failid/Patrik_Maldre_-_Global_Connections __Regional_Implications.pdf.

13. Pernik and Maldre, "Rising Challenges: Cybersecurity in the Baltic Sea Region."

14. NATO, "Cyber Defence Pledge," July 8, 2016, http://www.nato.int/cps/en/natohq/official_texts_133177.htm.

contingency) are still highly vulnerable in many places. A cyberattack could challenge "continuity of government operations, including utilities, telecommunications, transportation, and the financial system, as well as military command and control, which would pose a significant threat to the safety of ordinary citizens and government personnel."[15] Interlocutors we spoke with assessed that, while progress has been made in terms of recognizing the cyber threat, much more work is needed to build the resilience of national computer systems, especially as societies become increasingly digitalized and automated. The advanced digitalization of Baltic societies and economies was referenced in both Estonia and Lithuania as a characteristic that distinguishes the Baltics from Ukraine and Georgia, and which therefore raises the stakes on any Russian cyberattack against these countries. Experts in Poland also highlighted the heightened destructive power of cyberattacks in the age of the smartphone, with one Polish representative describing the most immediate threat as "not the enemy at the gates, [but] the enemy in your pocket."

Interlocutors in Poland also emphasized the need for greater synchronization between NATO and the European Union, and between the civilian and military sectors of national governments, in addition to less resistance to offensive cyber operations at the tactical level. On the latter point, participants at a working group in Poland bemoaned the political sensitivity surrounding offensive cyber operations, which they believe have the potential to helpfully shed light on Russia's cyber tactics, techniques, and procedures (TTPs).

CONVENTIONAL MILITARY IMBALANCE

By far the most concerning vulnerability to those we spoke with in the Baltic States and Poland was the conventional military imbalance between NATO and Russia along the eastern flank. Interlocutors in Latvia and Estonia, in particular, were hyperaware of the small size of their militaries, in addition to the superiority of the Russian military and the speed with which it could invade and conquer if so ordered. One expert concluded that "the sum total of what the Balts can muster buys a few days, if that."

A related, frequently expressed observation was the feeling that the governments of the Baltic States and Poland can likely "handle for [them]selves a hybrid 'little green men' scenario." There was an overall sense of confidence in the ability of regional governments to deal with low-intensity disturbances and a sense that national plans to resist such events have gained greatly in sophistication and robustness since 2014. There was near universal agreement, however, that—regardless of increased defense investment—the Baltics States and Poland will never be able to take on the Russians in a conventional matchup by themselves. As such, there was acknowledgment that they are reliant on the United States and NATO to provide "hard power" security guarantees. Therefore, much of the emphasis throughout our engagements was on the need for the United States and NATO to help backfill the conventional military capability and force gap between the eastern flank nations and Russia. According to residents, this should be accomplished through what was referred to as "day zero deterrence," obtained primarily by what was described as the

---

15. Kathleen H. Hicks, Heather A. Conley, et al. *Evaluating Future U.S. Army Force Posture in Europe* (Washington, DC: Center for Strategic and International Studies, June 2016), 68.

"3P's"—presence (of U.S. and other NATO forces), prepositioned equipment, and planning for contingencies. These requests will be discussed in greater detail in Section 3.

Aside from the sheer size and closeness of the Russian military, many interlocutors in the Baltic States and Poland expressed concern over the extensive Russian anti-access/area-denial (A2/AD) network that could prevent allies from being able to reinforce the region in an emergency; this is part of the reason why a credible in-place presence was considered so critical. An Estonian colleague described the Baltic States as a "strategic island" surrounded on one side by a layered missile architecture in the "Russian fortress of Kaliningrad" and on the other by a proliferation of advanced systems spanning the western edge of the Russian mainland. He added that "it would require a brave leader to take a risk and fly planes in anyway." Another observed that the current Russian missile array, combined with the absence of allied counter systems, means that "Russia can effectively cover all capitals from Sweden to Germany." They described Kaliningrad as a "window to the West," which gives Russia the ability to "control all lines of communication in the Baltic Sea."

Polish representatives also highlighted the vulnerability of the Suwalki Gap, the small area between Belarus and Kaliningrad that if conquered would essentially detach the Baltic States from the rest of the alliance. These same analysts felt that Belarus President Alexander Lukashenko, specifically, was being overestimated in terms of his ability to resist Russian demands for the use of Belarussian territory as a base for launching additional deep strikes at the West, noting that "Kaliningrad would not be enough." The Lithuanians we spoke with went further, claiming that the "Russian integration of Belarussian forces is nearly complete; they are the same forces with different uniforms."

Another aspect of the Russian military that stood out as a source of frequent concern was Moscow's continuing prioritization of defense modernization despite domestic economic challenges. There was a widespread perception that the Russian military is only getting better. Many interlocutors felt that Russia's actions in Ukraine—including its fusion of unmanned aerial systems and electronic warfare with precision targeting—demonstrate an increasing sophistication within the Russian force. There was broad agreement that, while still far from perfect, the Russian military had learned the lessons of its flawed 2008 operation in Georgia and, after studying the U.S. and NATO experience in Iraq and Afghanistan, had made smart investments in its military organization, capabilities, and TTPs. (It is also safe to assume that Russia is gathering and applying lessons from its most recent operations in Ukraine and Syria.) These advancements have been coupled with notable military posture adjustments near the Baltic region: the establishment of the Motorized Rifle Brigade in 2009 near the Estonian border; the reopening of the Ostrov Air Base near the Latvian border; and the placing of additional fighter jets at the Lida Air Base near the Belorussian-Lithuanian border.[16]

An additional source of concern was the frequency, locations, and scale at which Russia conducts large, no-notice "snap" exercises. NATO has accused Russia of using the exercises to

---

16. Ugis Romanovs, "The Means and Ends of Russia's Security Strategy," in *Security of the Broader Baltic Sea Region: Afterthoughts from the Riga Seminar*, ed. Andris Sprūds and Karlis Bukovskis (Riga: Latvian Institute of International Affairs, 2014), 44–50.

"deliberately avoid military transparency and predictability."[17] Several experts we spoke with from the region emphasized their fear that Russia's constant use of snap exercises would lead to a numbness among allies to massive Russian troop movements. In the words of one interviewee, "If the alert is constantly blinking red, we go off guard. This is when Russia will turn an exercise into an operation."

The Russian maritime threat was less frequently cited as a source for concern compared to Russia's land forces, though several military experts we spoke with flagged the growing capabilities of the Russian navy and NATO's "overemphasis on land." Polish participants felt it was increasingly important to protect against Russian infiltration through Gdansk Bay and noted the vulnerability of the undersea infrastructure crisscrossing the Baltic seafloor. Despite the concern, however, one regional American expert perceived a "general neglect of maritime across all the Baltic States" and Poland, partially as a result of American encouragement to focus on "creating caveat-free expeditionary infantry forces" as their contribution to the mission in Afghanistan.

The question, then, is not whether Russia *could* take the Baltics (the answer from participants was a resounding "yes"), but rather would they? Compared with most Western assessments that the likelihood of a Russian invasion of NATO territory is extremely low, the experts we spoke with from Estonia and Poland answered this question with much more skepticism. The Baltic States and Poland have had a long and violent history at the hands of the Russians; "we have no reason to trust [Russia]," explained one interlocutor. Many in the region felt a sense of validation following the events in Ukraine, noting that what the West sometimes viewed as undue paranoia was in fact justified cautious. Interlocutors were not shy in pointing out what they saw as the West's "fundamental misunderstanding [of Russia] and what deters [it]" and claiming that knowing Russia is their "comparative advantage." Still, our regional counterparts acknowledged that "Russia would have to make a high bet to go into a NATO country" and that Putin takes Article 5 seriously. In short, the likelihood of a Russian conventional invasion was still generally categorized as a low-probability event by those we spoke with, just not as low as the West generally assesses it to be.

OTHER VULNERABILITIES

A handful of other issues presented themselves in our review of the academic literature coming out of the region and in our conversations with regional experts. While mentioned with less overwhelming frequency and urgency than the issues discussed thus far, they nevertheless merit mentioning here. Among them, energy and economic dependence and interconnectedness with Russia were vulnerabilities that were both widely acknowledged as longer-term issues that will need to be addressed.

The energy sector is a weak point for several nations along NATO's eastern flank, although there are differences in the extent of dependence and vulnerability. The Lithuanians we spoke with were very proud that, for the first time since their independence, Russia was not Lithuania's top trading

---

17. NATO, "Statement by NATO Deputy Spokesperson Carmen Romero on NATO Military Exercises," August 12, 2015, http://www.nato.int/cps/en/natohq/news_122048.htm.

partner and that their country had diversified the vast majority of its energy imports away from Russian sources.[18] The other two Baltic States, particularly Latvia, have farther to go but are prioritizing efforts in this regard.

One of the more contentious energy issues in the region is the proposed NORD STREAM 2 project. Construction of this pipeline, a would-be joint operation between Russia's Gazprom and several European energy companies, would provide a second conduit for Russian energy to reach Europe and essentially allow Russia to bypass Ukraine. Lithuanian President Dalia Grybauskaite, the most vocally opposed among Baltic State leaders, stated that "[NORD STREAM 2] is a threat to the energy security of more than just Ukraine, it's a threat to all of Europe."[19] Likewise, the Poles we spoke with expressed anger and frustration regarding the proposed project, stating that it divides NATO and runs counter to the spirit of the sanctions put in place against Russia. They also noted their disappointment with NATO Secretary General Jens Stoltenberg's comments of February 23, 2016, which were perceived in Poland as essentially declaring that NORD STREAM 2 is not NATO's business:

> Well, I think it's something which has to be decided by the nations involved and to the extent it affects the European Union, decided by the European Union. It's not for NATO to decide whether it's good or bad to develop [NORD STREAM 2], so I think I have to leave that to the countries which are part of the project and to the extent it affects EU regulations, also the European Union.[20]

Lithuanian scholars have likewise pointed out NATO's natural tendency to focus on "hard" threats, as the alliance's traditional role is as a guarantor of territorial security, and to leave it to others to deal with the "soft" threats in the economic and energy sphere.[21] The majority of those we spoke with believe NATO should not abdicate "soft" security challenges completely to the EU or others, especially given the more immediate hybrid nature of the threat posed by Russia. Rather, they believe there is a need for ideas, including from the region, on how NATO-EU cooperation can advance a comprehensive security response to the Russian threat. Nuclear issues were also raised as a source of concern, which will be discussed more fully in Section 5.

---

18. Algirdas Butkevičius, "The Opening of the Croatian Embassy in Lithuania Will Strengthen the Partnership between Our Countries" (remarks, Vilnius, Lithuania, July 22, 2016), http://www.investineu.com/content/prime-minister -butkevi%C4%8Dius-opening-croatian-embassy-lithuania-will-strengthen-partnership-be.

19. "Grybauskaite—Gazprom Nord Stream 2 Gas Project Threatens European Energy Security," *Baltic Times*, December 8, 2015, http://www.baltictimes.com/grybauskaite_-_gazprom_nord_steam_2_gas_project_threatens_european _energy_security/.

20. Jens Stoltenberg, "Remarks at the European Parliament Committee on Foreign Affairs and Its Subcommittee on Security and Defence" (transcript, Brussels, Belgium, February 23, 2016), http://www.nato.int/cps/en/natohq/opinions _128311.htm?selectedLocale=en; "NATO: Nord Stream 2 to Nie Nasza Sprawa," *Energetyka24*, February 24, 2016, http:// www.energetyka24.com/314847,nato-nord-stream-2-to-nie-nasza-sprawa.

21. Arunas Molis and Gerda Jakstaite, "NATO's Transformation and Energy Security: The Perceptions and Role of a 'Newcomer,'" in *Newcomers No More? Contemporary NATO and the Future of Enlargement from the Perspective of "Post–Cold War" Members*, ed. Robert Czdulda and Marek Madej (Warsaw: International Relations Research Institute, 2015).

03

Regional Views of the U.S. and NATO Role in Conventional Deterrence

To gain a better understanding of regional expectations for allied response, the study team sought regional views on the eastern flank nations' relationships with the United States and NATO; the U.S. and European approach to reassurance following the Ukraine crisis; and the elements considered necessary for a credible conventional deterrence strategy. The experts we spoke with largely agreed that the United States and NATO needed to shift their emphasis from the assurance measures undertaken in the immediate aftermath of Russia's invasion of Ukraine to a longer-term strategy focused on defense and deterrence. As such, many discussions centered on the need for the forward deployment of U.S. and NATO military forces and war-fighting equipment to the Baltic States and Poland. Opinions varied, however, regarding the necessary size of the forces, the nature of their presence (i.e., rotational or permanent), and the additional capabilities that would be needed to deter Russia.

REGIONAL VIEWS OF THE UNITED STATES AND NATO

In general, our interlocutors in the Baltic States and Poland viewed their nations' security relationship with the United States as the safety net underwriting their defense and national security. Security relations with Washington were prioritized even above NATO and close neighbors. Forward-stationed U.S. forces in Europe, or American "boots on the ground," were seen as crucial elements of each nation's national security strategy. The primacy of U.S. security guarantees was not only evident in our discussions with regional experts and officials, but was codified in formal policy documents. Lithuania's national military strategy, for example, states, "The commitment of the United States to guarantee the security of the region and concrete measures of fulfilling this commitment are the key factors of the security of Lithuania."[1]

---

1. Ministry of National Defence of the Republic of Lithuania, "The Military Strategy of the Republic of Lithuania," March 17, 2016, 4, http://kam.lt/en/defence_policy_1053/important_documents/strategical_documents.html.

The importance placed by regional experts on the role of the United States in ensuring strategic stability on the eastern flank did not extend as acutely to NATO as an organization. While the Baltic States and Poland clearly value their membership in the alliance (along with their bilateral security ties with non-U.S. NATO allies), our discussions exposed an underlying skepticism toward the timeliness of NATO's decisionmaking mechanisms and, relatedly, pervasive doubts regarding the level of political will that would be needed to reach a consensus for action. As one participant stated, "We cannot fall hostage to NATO consensus." Our discussions also revealed resentment of a perceived Western assumption that defense of the Baltics is impossible and that a fight for liberation after a successful Russian invasion and occupation would most likely be required. In such a case, several interlocutors questioned whether allies would fight at all and, moreover, whether Article 5 could really be relied on in an alliance-wide context. Given Russia's proximity to the eastern flank, several commentators, particularly those in the Baltic States, viewed any delay in allied reaction time as the difference between their extermination and survival. Most felt that the stakes in such a scenario were too high to put blind faith in NATO and that the only viable and capable-enough first responder is the United States. They felt that second- and third-wave reinforcements from NATO would be important, of course, but only if Russia's initial onslaught could be successfully weathered.

Participants' concerns regarding the commitment of NATO (as an organization) to rapidly respond to a threat from Russia are perhaps understandable. A June 2015 poll conducted by the Pew Research Center surveyed publics in eight of the largest NATO countries—the United States, Germany, France, the United Kingdom, Poland, Italy, Spain, and Canada—regarding whether their nation should intervene militarily in the case of Russian aggression against a NATO ally.[2] Six out of the eight countries surveyed failed to deliver a majority opinion that their country should intervene against Russian aggression, while a majority in three countries—Italy, Germany, and France—stated that the country should not support its allies. An overwhelming number of those we spoke with in the Baltic States and Poland emphasized the importance of the United States' leadership role within NATO. There was a belief that action by NATO would ultimately hinge on U.S. leaders being able to forge consensus and prod allies into action.

REGIONAL VIEWS TOWARD POST-UKRAINE ASSURANCE EFFORTS

Baltic and Polish interlocutors were encouraged by U.S. reassurance efforts taken since 2014 under the auspices of Operation Atlantic Resolve (OAR). The most significant effort under OAR has been the persistent presence of a U.S. Army company in Poland and each Baltic State, in addition to prepositioned equipment and periodic rotations of U.S. air and naval forces to the region. Most observers from the region and Washington saw the continued presence of U.S. forces on the

---

2. Katie Simmons, Bruce Stokes, and Jacob Poushter, "NATO Publics Blame Russia for Ukrainian Crisis, but Reluctant to Provide Military Aid: In Russia, Anti-Western Views and Support for Putin Surge," Pew Research Center, June 2015, http://www.pewglobal.org/2015/06/10/nato-publics-blame-russia-for-ukrainian-crisis-but-reluctant-to-provide -military-aid/.

eastern flank to be necessary to ensure stability and viewed these deployments as the starting point for a longer-term and enhanced forward presence.

Regional observers were likewise grateful for the solidarity shown by NATO in the wake of the Ukraine crisis, though were less enthusiastic by comparison when it came to non-U.S. NATO assurance measures. Much of their disappointment was related to the alliance's failure to fully realize its original vision for the Very High Readiness Joint Task Force (VJTF), NATO's new "spear-head" rapid response force announced at the 2014 Wales Summit.[3] As originally conceived, the VJTF was intended to go beyond the rapid response forces already resident within the NATO Response Force (NRF) by (1) further shortening deployment timelines and (2) delegating additional authorities to NATO's Supreme Allied Commander (SACEUR) in times of crisis. Neither change, however, could reach consensus at the level certain eastern flank nations viewed as minimally sufficient. In the opinion of several regional experts, the watered-down nature of the VJTF ultimately fails to overcome Russia's so-called time and space advantage in a challenge that they see as mostly about speed. One regional participant even dismissed the VJTF as a "fantasy construct." Adding to these concerns, experts in Estonia and Lithuania pointed out that the threat of Russian A2/AD capabilities could render the deployment of the VJTF to the northeastern flank nearly impossible at the outset of a crisis, making it more viable as a follow-on reinforcement force, not a first responder.

As previously mentioned, regional interlocutors also expressed concern that continued provocations by Moscow would dull U.S. and allied alertness and that there was already some sense of complacency setting in as the urgency prompted by the Ukraine crisis faded with time. Given that the threat posed by Moscow is not diminishing, however, they felt that shifting from assurance to deterrence—by emplacing a capable and robust on-the-ground presence—was needed.

SHIFTING TO CONVENTIONAL DETERRENCE

Our dialogues in the region and in Washington took place between March and May 2016 amid a debate within NATO and the United States over the establishment of an enhanced, forward, allied troop presence on the eastern flank. In February 2016, NATO defense ministers agreed in principle to create an enhanced forward presence of multinational troops on the eastern flank to deter Russia. The details of the presence, however, remained unresolved and were being negotiated in the months before the Warsaw Summit in July 2016.[4] Taking place as they did in the run-up to Warsaw, our discussions thus lend important insights into the final decision.

At the Warsaw Summit, NATO leaders announced their decision to deploy one NATO-flagged battalion per country to Poland, Estonia, Latvia, and Lithuania, for a total of four.[5] Each battalion (made up of approximately 800 to 1,000 troops) will be led by a framework nation, with the United

---

3. NATO, "NATO's Readiness Action Plan," fact sheet, October 2015, http://www.nato.int/nato_static_fl2014/assets/pdf/pdf_2015_12/20151130_1512-factsheet_rap_en.pdf.

4. NATO, "NATO Boosts Its Defence and Deterrence Posture," February 11, 2016, http://www.nato.int/cps/en/natohq/news_127834.htm.

5. NATO, "Warsaw Summit Communiqué."

States taking the lead in Poland, Germany in Lithuania, Canada in Latvia, and the United Kingdom in Estonia. While the framework nation will contribute the bulk of the forces, other NATO allies are also expected to contribute forces that will round out each battlegroup. As these NATO battalions are put in place, the rotational U.S. Army companies deployed to the Baltic States under OAR are likely to be consolidated and then rotate through the eastern flank to conduct training events and participate in exercises. U.S. training equipment that is currently prepositioned on the eastern flank will be gradually withdrawn to Western Europe and modified to become war-fighting stocks. With the outcome in mind, we can assess whether the outcome agreed at Warsaw met the expectations of eastern flank allies as expressed to our study team.

Our interactions with regional representatives highlighted a strong desire to see the United States and NATO shift toward a conventional deterrence posture on the eastern flank. Several experts we spoke with equated deterrence strategy with a stalwart forward defense of the Baltics. There was, however, a variety of opinions on the composition and strength of the forces that would be needed along the eastern flank to effectively deter Russia. As explained in Section 2, discussions in this regard tended to focus on the steps needed to deter Russian aggression in the form of a high-end conventional attack, with less emphasis on how to deter so-called hybrid threats. Observers' remarks were therefore concentrated on the need for allied conventional forces and the related questions of force size, positioning, weapons systems and capabilities, rules of engagement, and other elements of combined military responses. There was significantly less emphasis on how to best deter low-end hybrid threats or whether a conventional deterrence strategy could be tailored to address the diverse set of threats facing the eastern flank.

Most participants tended toward ambiguity regarding the size of U.S. and allied forces they believed were needed to establish a credible deterrent. Instead of offering specifics, those we spoke with emphasized the need for a forward presence that was "sufficiently combat capable." The maintenance of a persistent U.S. troop presence was a clear priority. Some interlocutors expressed worry that U.S. forces might be replaced rather than augmented by other allied troops when NATO moved ahead with its enhanced forward presence. This did not detract from the desire for non-U.S. NATO troop deployments in addition to U.S. forces, however, in order to "get as many flags as possible." Still, while regional defense experts and U.S. participants agreed that multinational forces were useful in maximizing force structure, there was also agreement that integrating too many small units from multiple allies could create interoperability problems and would require unwieldy command-and-control structures. It was made clear that the force needed to be credible above all else.

Regarding a permanent versus a rotational presence, regional interlocutors were generally resigned to stop fighting Western allies' reluctance to permanently deploy forces to the Baltic States and Poland, though they continued to disagree with the logic of the decision. From their perspective, Western objections to permanent stationing on the basis of the NATO-Russia Founding Act (NRFA)—which they see Russia as having invalidated through its own violations of the Act—only reward and further enable Russian rule-breaking.[6] Polish participants were more vocal than their

---

6. NATO-Russia Founding Act states, "NATO reiterates that in the current and foreseeable security environment, the Alliance will carry out its collective defence and other missions by ensuring the necessary interoperability, integration,

Baltic counterparts in the belief that the NRFA should be nullified and in expressing a strong preference for the permanent stationing of U.S. troops in Poland, echoing calls from the Polish president for "as permanent a presence as possible."[7] While many of our Baltic interlocutors also indicated a preference for permanently stationed U.S. and allied forces, those we spoke with were more acquiescent to the perceived political realities that made such a decision impossible. In the end, all conceded that rotational forces were sufficient as long as they were continuous, "heel-to-toe" deployments.

Based on our dialogues, the Baltic States and Poland are likely quite satisfied with the final outcome of the Warsaw Summit. The establishment of an enhanced forward (rotational) presence of approximately 1,000 NATO troops in each country is a significant commitment of forces and resources and underscores a shift by the alliance toward a deterrence posture. Estonian Prime Minister Taavi Roivas described the decisions made at Warsaw as "a breakthrough that unambiguously demonstrates NATO's solidarity and the fact that Estonia is better protected today than ever before."[8] Leaders from across the region have likewise made positive statements regarding NATO's decisions.[9] Over the long term, the Baltic States and Poland are likely to continue to push for priority on eastern flank challenges and press for the new battle groups to remain fully manned and combat capable.

---

and capability for reinforcement rather than by additional permanent stationing of substantial combat forces." NATO, "Founding Act on Mutual Relations, Cooperation and Security between NATO and the Russian Federation Signed in Paris, France," last modified October 12, 2016, http://www.nato.int/cps/en/natohq/official_texts_25468.htm.

7. Julian E. Barnes, "Polish President Calls for Visible NATO Force," *Wall Street Journal*, January 18, 2016, http://www.wsj.com/articles/polish-president-calls-for-visible-nato-force-in-poland-1453128541.

8. "Estonian PM: Decision to Increase NATO Presence Is Breakthrough," *Baltic Times*, July 7, 2016, http://www.baltictimes.com/estonian_pm__decision_to_increase_nato_presence_is_breakthrough/.

9. See "Prime Minister Szydło hails NATO summit success for Poland," *Radio Poland*, July 11, 2016, http://www.thenews.pl/1/10/Artykul/261227,Prime-Minister-Szydlo-hails-NATO-summit-success-for-Poland; Richard Milne, "Lithuania Welcomes NATO Deployment of Troops," *Financial Times*, July 3, 2016, http://www.ft.com/cms/s/0/13a8de5e-3f7b-11e6-8716-a4a71e8140b0.html#axzz4EsdnsoAc; Matthew Fisher, "Latvians Welcome Tiny Canadian Force to Help Dissuade Russia's Military Adventurism," *National Post*, July 8, 2016, http://news.nationalpost.com/news/world/matthew-fisher-latvians-welcome-tiny-canadian-force-to-help-dissuade-russias-military-adventurism.

04

Regional Approaches to Internal Defense and Security

Despite dramatic differences in size, budgets, and capabilities, the Baltic and Polish militaries all share a heavy emphasis on land forces within their defense structures, generally to the exclusion of coastal defense and maritime investments (as well as air power in the Baltic States). While Poland has been able to build capacity across a broader spectrum of defense requirements, the Baltic States have sought to compensate for deficiencies in scope and scale by contributing in small but meaningful ways to international operations; offering robust host-nation support to visiting forces; and cultivating specialties and niche capabilities—for example, cyber defense in Estonia, joint terminal attack controllers and explosive ordnance disposal in Latvia, and special operations forces in Lithuania—that can provide a qualitative benefit to NATO.

Communist legacies related to defense organization, procurement, and personnel remain a challenge for Poland. The challenge faced by the Baltic militaries, however, was different: they were largely reconstituted from the ground up following the end of the Soviet occupation, during which the Red Army had disbanded the national defense forces.[1] All face struggles in building a credible deterrent against Russian aggression. All have committed to increasing defense investments and are undertaking steps to better integrate their internal security, intelligence, and defense forces, though the pace of reform varies by country. In general, the Baltic States would benefit from better synchronization in defense planning and procurement across national lines as well as reinforced internal national guard structures.

Officials and experts we spoke with were disappointed at the lack of military coordination among the Baltic States. While Baltic leaders acknowledge that any weak link among them will only increase the exposure and risk to all three, common defense planning remains stifled by the region's difficult strategic geography and the need to prioritize small military forces around self-defense. The result is independent defense and contingency plans.

---

1. See Daunis Auers, *Comparative Politics and Government of the Baltic States: Estonia, Latvia, and Lithuania in the 21st Century* (London: Palgrave Macmillan, 2015).

Likewise, while the Baltic States are supportive of joint procurement initiatives in theory, differences in budget timelines, capability priorities, preferred hardware configurations, and political circumstances have inhibited the full realization of a joint approach and the cost efficiencies found therein. Ammunition is one of the few areas where Baltic militaries have been able to come together in a joint procurement arrangement, though there are ongoing discussions between Latvia and Lithuania for medium-range air defenses that could usefully expand cooperation. The discounts available through the purchase of secondhand or thirdhand equipment are also contributing to competition between the Baltic States rather than cooperation. Regarding Poland, according to the experts we spoke with, the country is similarly not philosophically opposed to joint procurement programs, assuming they introduce economies of scale. Such programs have been stymied, however, by availability issues for major purchases, and by Poland's insistence that any purchase directly benefit the Polish defense industry.

The Baltic States are also focused on improving the capacity and readiness of their volunteer national guard structures, which have taken on renewed importance since 2014. Baltic defense experts interviewed for this report emphasized the important roles that the Estonian Defence League, the Latvian National Guard, and the Lithuanian National Defence Volunteer Forces each play in the Baltic States' national contingency plans given the small number of standing forces. Most, however, expressed concern regarding their training, equipping, and readiness. Given the lack of territorial depth and the proximity of Russian forces at the onset of any crisis, military mobilization in the Baltic States must be extremely rapid and well-rehearsed. These experts worried that senior government officials in the region were overestimating the abilities of the volunteer national guards to the detriment of approaching reforms with necessary urgency.

The following sections offer more specifics on the internal defense structures of each of the three Baltic States and Poland, as well as their individual approaches to enhancing deterrence and prioritizing capability requirements.

ESTONIA

Since Russia's aggression against Ukraine in 2014, Estonia has embarked on efforts to expand and better equip its small active-duty ground forces while standing up additional reserve and national guard forces. The Estonian Defence Forces (EDF) are the smallest active-duty military in the Baltic States, numbering approximately 3,200 personnel—with 2,800 active-duty professional soldiers in the army, 200 in the navy, and 250 in the air force.[2] While Estonia spends 2 percent of its gross domestic product (GDP) on defense, this amounts to only $490 million annually due to the country's small size.[3]

---

2. This figure does not include the 2,500 conscripts in the army, as conscript units are placed in reserve upon completion of their training; see International Institute for Strategic Studies (IISS), *The Military Balance 2016* (London: Routledge, 2016), 91. See also Estonian Defence Forces, "Compulsory Military Service," November 3, 2014, http://www.mil.ee/en /defence-forces/compulsory-military-service.

3. NATO, "Defence Expenditures of NATO Countries (2009–2016)," press release, July 4, 2016, http://www.nato.int /nato_static_fl2014/assets/pdf/pdf_2016_07/20160704_160704-pr2016-116.pdf.

The Estonian Land Force, the primary service branch, is largely structured as a reserve military geared toward territorial defense. The land forces are spearheaded by a light infantry scouts battalion and a small special operations force (SOF) component. These two units—the only active-duty formations manned by professional soldiers—maintain a high degree of readiness and have regularly deployed with NATO forces overseas. The remainder of Estonia's land forces, approximately 3,200 conscripts, are structured as a reserve force of two light infantry brigades. A primary role for the active-duty personnel, therefore, is to organize, train, and equip the largely conscript reservists who must be able to quickly mobilize in the event of a crisis. Supplementing the small regular military is the Estonian Defence League (EDL), a volunteer national paramilitary organization with approximately 15,000 volunteers.[4]

Estonians are proud to be one of only five NATO countries, along with Poland, to meet NATO's defense spending benchmark of 2 percent of GDP. Interlocutors expressed concerns, however, that without spending beyond 2 percent, Estonia would face serious challenges bridging many of its most glaring capability gaps, including sufficient air surveillance radars, short-range air defenses, coastal defenses, adequate munition stockpiles, and basic infantry equipment to outfit new reserve units and the EDL. Still, the Estonian Defence Force is making some headway with these requirements and is in the process of procuring Dutch CV-90 Infantry Fighting Vehicles, Javelin antitank guided missiles, tactical unmanned aerial systems, and basic equipment for the EDL and reserve forces, including rifles and munitions.

While interlocutors spoke highly of the abilities of Estonia's scouts battalion and SOF, which have operated alongside U.S. and NATO forces in Iraq and Afghanistan without caveats, as well as Tallinn's cyber capabilities, numerous discussions revealed concerns about the state of readiness of the reserve units and the EDL. Interviewees indicated that the actual number of trained, equipped, and capable personnel in the EDL was likely in the hundreds, a far cry from the 15,000 cited by official government sources. Estonia was, however, able to muster 7,000 reservists as part of the 13,000-troop strong force comprised of members of the active force, reserves, and EDL for a two-week exercise—Estonia's largest ever—to test the nation's readiness to repel a Russian invasion.[5] The exercise, Siil 2015 (Hedgehog 2015), is aptly named as much of the Baltic States' defense strategies rests on making themselves, in the words of one official, "as prickly as possible for Russia to swallow" in order to buy time for allied reinforcements to arrive.

4. Estonian Defence League, "Estonian Defence League," August 10, 2016, http://www.kaitseliit.ee/en/edl.

5. S. Tambur, "Estonia's Largest-Ever Military Exercise Involving 13,000 Soldiers Kicks Off," Estonian Public Broadcasting, April 5, 2015, http://news.err.ee/v/news/defense/6620af7b-cc70-4742-a228-4c0324269243/estonias-largest-ever-military-exercise-involving-13000-soldiers-kicks-off; Ben Farmer, "Estonia Stages Biggest Military Exercise in Country's History amid Fears of Russian 'Aggression,'" Telegraph, May 12, 2015, http://www.telegraph.co.uk/news/worldnews/europe/estonia/11600458/Estonia-stages-biggest-military-exercise-in-countrys-history-amid-fears-of-Russian-aggression.html.

LATVIA

At 1.4 percent of GDP, or about $380 million in 2016, Latvia has been increasing its defense spending annually since 2014 and aims to reach NATO's 2 percent target by 2018.[6] The Latvian National Armed Forces is an all-volunteer military composed of 4,700 active-duty personnel with approximately 1,200 in the army and 2,600 joint personnel assigned to SOF and enabler units. Latvia's ground forces are comprised of two infantry battalions and a SOF component. The small regular military is buttressed by the Latvian National Guard, a volunteer paramilitary force with approximately 8,000 members.[7] Acquisition priorities for Latvia include air surveillance radars, antitank guided missiles, armored fighting vehicles, and short-range air defense systems.

Interlocutors in Riga generally expressed concern at the scale and speed of the reform measures undertaken by Riga in recent years to enhance its security forces. While complimentary of the performance of Latvian forces in exercises and the government's decision to increase defense spending, local exerts believed the Latvian government was overly optimistic regarding the sufficiency of its force structure, capabilities, and state of readiness. Much of the criticism focused on the Latvian National Guard, with one member of the organization stating that only half of its 8,000 members could be considered at least partially viable for resistance in an emergency, while also describing a worrying lack of structure and equipment. Several interlocutors suggested that Latvia's defense spending would likely need to increase faster and likely beyond 2 percent of GDP, alongside continuing reforms within the ministries of defense and interior, in order to have sufficiently robust and resilient security forces able to respond to low-intensity crises.

LITHUANIA

Lithuania has the largest military of the three Baltic States, owing to its larger economy and population, and is similarly structured around territorial defense, with the Lithuanian Land Force (LLF) serving as the predominant service. While Lithuania does not share a border with mainland Russia like Estonia and Latvia, it does touch the Russian enclave of Kaliningrad to its west and Belarus—which Russian forces could cross (with or without the sanction of the Belarusian leadership)—to its east. Lithuanian defenses therefore need to be oriented against potential threats from either direction. Moreover, Lithuania's terrain is generally more open and flat than its northern Baltic counterparts, making territorial defense against conventional threats all the more challenging. Lithuania's defense budget in 2016 is $1.67 billion, amounting to 1.5 percent of GDP. While still falling below NATO's spending target, Lithuania has rapidly increased its defense spending since the crisis in Ukraine in 2014, almost doubling spending from 0.8 percent of GDP in 2013, with plans to reach 2 percent by 2018.

---

6. Latvian Ministry of Defence, "Government Defence Priorities," March 2016, http://www.mod.gov.lv/Par_aizsardzibas _nozari/Politikas_planosana/Vald_priorit.aspx.

7. Latvia forces have developed niche capability areas to support NATO overseas deployments including Joint Tactical Air Control (JTAC) and Explosive Ordinance Disposal (EOD) capabilities.

The active component of the LLF is manned by approximately 6,000 professional soldiers and 4,800 active reservists.[8] The primary fighting component of the LLF is the Iron Wolf brigade, a mechanized infantry force comprised of four infantry battalions and an artillery battalion.[9] Defense officials have recognized the need to increase the LLF's force structure and in 2016 began establishing a second motorized infantry brigade that will incorporate two previously independent motorized infantry battalions and two entirely new battalions.[10] To help support the growth in the LLF's force structure, Lithuania reintroduced compulsory military service in 2015. Beyond force structure enhancements, Lithuania is spending its increased defense investment on new capabilities. It is seeking to modernize its forces with self-propelled artillery systems, infantry fighting vehicles, short-range air defense systems, aerial surveillance systems, logistics vehicles, and anti-tank guided missiles.[11]

POLAND

The Polish Armed Forces (PAF) are by far the most robust and capable military on NATO's eastern flank. Upon joining NATO in 1999, Poland focused on transforming its large and heavy Soviet-style military into a smaller and lighter expeditionary force capable of deploying and fighting alongside U.S. and allied forces, contributions viewed by Warsaw as a critical pillar for Poland's national security. The PAF has undertaken a number of crucial reforms since 1999, including transitioning from a conscript military to an all-volunteer, professional force; integrating Western military equipment into its inventory; and restructuring its bloated, top-heavy military organization into a leaner, more agile joint fighting force.

Poland gradually began shifting its military's focus from external crisis management back to territorial defense as relations with Moscow soured following the Russia-Georgia War in 2008 and the Smolensk plane crash in 2010, and as its confidence in Washington was tested following the Obama administration's 2009 decision to scale back its planned deployment of missile defenses

8. Vytautas Jokubauskas, "The Financing and Personnel of the Lithuanian Army," *Lithuanian Annual Strategic Review* 13 (2014–2015): 147–170, http://www.degruyter.com/downloadpdf/j/lasr.2015.13.issue-1/lasr-2015-0008/lasr-2015 -0008.xml; Agne Cepinskyte, "Lithuania Reinstates Conscription: Implications on Security, National Identity, and Gender Roles" Foreign Policy Research Institute, June 6, 2016, http://www.fpri.org/article/2016/06/lithuania-reinstates -conscription-implications-security-national-identity-gender-roles/.

9. "Mechanized Infantry Brigade 'Iron Wolf,'" Lithuanian Armed Forces, last modified March 3, 2016, https://kariuomene .kam.lt/en/structure_1469/land_force/structure_1299.html.

10. "Lithuania Increases the Army," *Baltic Review*, January 3, 2016, http://baltic-review.com/lithuania-increases-the -army/; Lithuanian Ministry of National Defence, "A New Brigade Named Žemaitija Is Established within the Lithuanian Armed Forces in Western Lithuania," press release, December 31, 2015, http://www.kam.lt/en/news_1098/current _issues/a_new_brigade_named_zemaitija_is_established_within_the_lithuanian_armed_forces_in_western_lithuania .html?pbck=10.

11. Jakub Palowski, "German Boxer APCs Acquired by Lithuania," *Defence24*, December 14, 2015, http://www .defence24.com/281795,german-boxer-apcs-acquired-by-lithuania-armed-with-spike-anti-tank-guided-missiles.

to Poland.[12] Beginning in 2013, Poland embarked on an ambitious 10-year, $35 billion modernization effort with major investments in integrated air and missile defense systems, helicopters, submarines, armored vehicles, unmanned aerial vehicles, and command-and-control systems, in addition to upgrades for its main battle tanks and fighter aircraft.[13] By 2015, Poland's defense budget had reached approximately $10.5 billion, or about 2 percent of GDP, making it one of five NATO members, along with Estonia, to reach the alliance's defense spending target.[14]

Poland's military is comprised of approximately 100,000 active-duty personnel, the vast majority of which belong to the land forces (77,000 personnel and 13 maneuver brigades). The bulk of the PAF are based in western Poland near the German border, a legacy of Poland's Cold War posture, while many units based in the eastern provinces remain undermanned. Few regular forces are located in proximity to the Suwalki Gap—the narrow land corridor to Lithuania bordered by Kaliningrad and Belarus that many Polish interlocutors considered the most likely entry point for Russia soldiers in the event of an invasion. To augment its force structure and rebalance its forces to the north and east, Poland plans to create three territorial defense brigades manned by up to 20,000 reservists, which would be tasked with securing key infrastructure and lines of communication.

Poland will face a number of long-term obstacles as it seeks to modernize its defense capabilities. While Poland began updating its military stocks with Western equipment after joining NATO, much of the PAF remains reliant on aging Soviet-era hardware. As new equipment comes on line, the higher per-unit costs as well as larger maintenance, sustainment, and training costs will force trade-offs between modern capabilities and additional force structure, both of which Poland views as necessary for credible deterrence.[15] Polish Minister of Defence Antoni Macierewicz has called for Poland to further increase its defense spending to 3 percent of GDP, seemingly to avoid such trade-offs, although such an increase seems politically unachievable.[16]

Experts with knowledge of the country's procurement practices expressed concerns that Warsaw is pursuing modernization efforts than it could neither afford nor properly manage. They explained that Poland has a tendency to buy bare-bones equipment packages to bring down costs, only to later discover that the critical systems it opted out of were necessary to meet military requirements, thus necessitating further upgrades at higher cost. In other cases, they pointed out, Poland has neglected to put in place adequate sustainment and logistics agreements needed to properly maintain its new equipment. For example, Poland purchased 128 surplus Leopard 2A5 tanks from

---

12. In discussions, it was Polish experts and officials who raised the notion that Poland's shift toward territorial defense also began as a reaction to the Obama administration's 2009 decision to scuttle plans to deploy ballistic missile interceptors in the country, which Warsaw viewed as a major setback.

13. Jaroslaw Adamowski, "Poland Plans to Spend $21B on Drones, Helos, Air Defense, Subs," *Defense News*, July 20, 2016, http://www.defensenews.com/story/defense/2016/07/20/poland-plans-spending-21-billion-helos-air-defense-systems-submarines-uavs/87341052/.

14. NATO, "Defence Expenditures of NATO Countries."

15. Tomasz Szatkowski, "Budget Implications of Poland's Pivot to Territorial Defence," *European Leadership Network*, February 9, 2015, http://www.europeanleadershipnetwork.org/budget-implications-of-polands-pivot-to-territorial-defence_2413.html.

16. "Poland to Increase Military Budget," *Ukraine Today*, July 11, 2016, http://uatoday.tv/politics/poland-to-increase-military-budget-693237.html.

Germany in 2013 but failed to acquire technical documentation for the tanks or develop sufficient plans for their maintenance and overhaul, which caused significant delays in the modernization of its tank forces.[17] Similarly, Poland's F-16 fleet was troubled by maintenance issues for several years due to chronic shortages of spare parts and other issues.[18] While not unusual, Poland's customary insistence on joint production contracts and technology transfers to support and develop its largely state-owned defense industry was noted as another frequent source of procurement delays and complication.

Beyond reforming force structure and procurement practices, overcoming the communist legacy within the defense bureaucracy continues to pose a challenge. Civilian control over the PAF was formally codified in 1997—two years before Poland joined NATO. While civil-military relations in Poland have advanced by leaps and bounds since, the Polish military's deep politicization under the communist regime and its role in the crackdown against the Solidarity movement has left lingering chords of distrust between today's civilian leaders and senior military officers who were trained during the communist era. Interlocutors we spoke with also pointed out that continued politicization, albeit less pronounced, of promotions and assignments for senior officers negatively impacts morale and places inexperienced officers in senior positions.

---

17. Antoni Macierewicz, "Report on the State of Public Affairs and State Institutions as of the End of PO-PSL Coalition Rule" (speech, Polonia Institute, Warsaw, Poland, May 11, 2016), https://www.poloniainstitute.net/expert-analyses/security-policy/the-speech-of-antoni-macierewicz-the-minister-of-national-defense-of-the-republic-of-poland/.

18. Aaron Mehta, "Poland Eyes F-16 Sustainment Change," *Defense News*, June 3, 2016, http://www.defensenews.com/story/defense-news/2016/06/03/poland-f-16-sustainment-aesa-radar/85350178/.

05

The Nuclear Dimension on the Eastern Flank

Nuclear deterrence was an essential element in NATO policy and posture throughout the Cold War and remains so to this day. The alliance as an organization does not possess any nuclear weapons in its own right; rather, strategic deterrence is provided by the individual members with such capabilities—the United States, the United Kingdom, and France (though France's arsenal remains technically outside of NATO's nuclear framework)—and by the burden sharing of nonnuclear allies. While NATO has reduced the role of nuclear weapons since the end of the Cold War—and while the United States has reduced the number and types of its nuclear systems deployed in Europe—nuclear weapons, especially the U.S. strategic arsenal, remain the ultimate guarantee of NATO's security.[1]

As NATO confronts the threat from a resurgent Russia, most of the alliance's focus since 2014 has been on strengthening conventional deterrence through the rotational deployment of land forces. There is a growing chorus of allies, however, calling for greater attention on the nuclear component of the alliance's deterrent.[2] In their view, Russia's troubling pattern of nuclear saber rattling—including targeting Poland and the Baltic States with nuclear weapons in military exercises—and the role these weapons play in Russian attempts at coercion requires a renewed NATO focus on nuclear deterrence. Russia's actions since the Ukraine crisis have included direct and implied statements designed to intimidate individual NATO allies and neighbors with Russia's nuclear capabilities. Moscow also has tried to delegitimize NATO's nuclear sharing arrangements. Observers in the Baltic States and Poland were especially concerned that Russia may be lowering its threshold for using its nuclear weapons. This concern results in part from ambiguity in Russia's

1. NATO, "Strategic Concept for the Defence and Security of the Members of the North Atlantic Treaty Organization," November 19–20, 2010, http://www.nato.int/nato_static_fl2014/assets/pdf/pdf_publications/20120214_strategic-concept-2010-eng.pdf.

2. Dmitry Adamsky, "Cross-Domain Coercion: The Current Russian Art of Strategy," Institut Français des Relations Internationales Proliferation Papers 54 (November 2015), http://www.ifri.org/sites/default/files/atoms/files/pp54adamsky.pdf.

nuclear policy—in particular, the possibility that Russia could envision a "de-escalatory" nuclear strike in conjunction with conventional aggression on the eastern flank of NATO.[3]

Russia's published national security strategy and military doctrine officially contemplate nuclear strikes only in response to use of weapons of mass destruction against Russia or in a situation where Russia's very existence is threatened.[4] However, counterparts were uncertain (1) how Russia would define a threat to its existence; (2) whether there are classified elements of its nuclear doctrine that contradict the published strategies; and (3) whether Russia's political leadership would conform to doctrine in a crisis or seek to project unpredictability as a way to help it prevail. They add that the danger of proliferation outside the Euro-Atlantic region, combined with growing nuclear forces in countries already possessing such weapons, further underscores the need for NATO to reemphasize its nuclear deterrent.

In general, analysts in the Baltic States and Poland viewed the nuclear challenge as fundamentally political—a threat intended to raise the stakes and divide NATO allies. Russia would succeed only if it weakened allied solidarity sufficiently to render NATO unable to respond to Russian aggression. From their perspective, a political challenge requires, first and foremost, a political response—to convince Russia (or any other potential nuclear adversary) that there is no reasonable prospect of fracturing alliance unity and that crossing the nuclear threshold would invite incalculable risks. Counterparts in all countries identified a need for a stronger NATO declaratory stance on nuclear issues in light of Russia's threatening rhetoric and irresponsible behavior.

Beyond declaratory measures, there were differences of emphasis on further steps NATO should take. Some in the Baltic States and Poland suggested a strengthened nuclear posture. Others argued to incorporate more nuclear scenarios into NATO exercises and to develop graduated response options. There were also calls to consider including central European allies in NATO's nuclear sharing arrangements by developing their dual-capable aircraft capabilities. These aircraft could be based, they thought, in countries that already host U.S. tactical nuclear weapons, thereby not requiring the basing of nuclear weapons or delivery platforms on the territory of newer members. Alternatively, a minority view held that the deployment of NATO forces to the eastern flank, along with other measures to strengthen conventional deterrence, actually minimized the need for an enhanced nuclear posture given that nuclear weapons were no longer necessarily needed to compensate for conventional weakness.

U.S. participants emphasized the need to revitalize the discussion of NATO's nuclear deterrent, which has largely receded from public consciousness since the end of the Cold War. With nuclear threats playing a frequent role in Russian attempts to intimidate its neighbors, it was seen as vital

---

3. For an analysis of Russia's approach to nuclear weapons, changes in doctrine since the end of the Cold War, and whether "de-escalatory" nuclear use is envisioned by Russia, see Olga Oliker, *Russia's Nuclear Doctrine: What We Know, What We Don't, and What That Means* (Washington, DC: Center for Strategic and International Studies, 2016), https://csis-prod.s3.amazonaws.com/s3fs-public/publication/160504_Oliker_RussiasNuclearDoctrine_Web.pdf.

4. Russian Federation, "National Security Strategy of the Russian Federation," December 2015, http://static.kremlin.ru/media/events/files/ru/l8iXkR8XLAtxeilX7JK3XXy6Y0AsHD5v.pdf; Russian Federation, "Military Doctrine of the Russian Federation," December 2014, https://www.offiziere.ch/wp-content/uploads-001/2015/08/Russia-s-2014-Military-Doctrine.pdf.

that public understanding and support for NATO's nuclear policy remain solid. Representatives of the eastern flank countries saw this as a less pressing issue given their belief that their particular populations were more keenly aware and supportive of the role nuclear deterrence played in alliance security. Regardless, all agreed that if enhanced public discourse strengthened solidarity among European allies, and in particular in the basing countries, it would have a clear benefit.

The operational posture and modernization of nuclear forces, including delivery platforms, was also a priority from the viewpoint of American experts, as was allied burden sharing. Sustaining broad participation in the nuclear mission was seen as crucial to alliance cohesion, including, for example, pending decisions in some allied nations on dual-capable aircraft that are part of NATO's nuclear mission. Greater participation by nonnuclear allies in NATO nuclear exercises would likewise demonstrate concrete action by allies to deepen the credibility of this assurance.[5]

There was also a pervasive atmosphere of unease and mistrust among those we spoke with re-garding Russia's denial that it is in violation of the Intermediate-Range Nuclear Forces (INF) Treaty. According to our interlocutors, Russia's deceit on this issue undermines productive dialogue and transparency measures meant to manage risk across a broader range of issues. Polish counter-parts felt that the INF violation justified "tough language and consequences." While the violation does not affect the strategic balance between the United States and Russia, it does raise the possibility that most European territory could become vulnerable to nuclear strikes from advanced Russian cruise missiles, thus increasing the pressure within NATO to develop a commensurate response.

There was a reluctance among most Washington analysts to advocate developing capabilities that match tit-for-tat all of Russia's purported capabilities. They preferred to instead focus on retaining the ability to impose overwhelming costs on an adversary. They thought the central role of the U.S. arsenal in NATO strategic deterrence provides credibility without requiring a mirroring of Russian capabilities or activity. Besides, they argued, a shift in U.S. or NATO nuclear policy could also entail political risks, as it might raise fears in NATO electorates (especially in basing countries) that NATO—rather than Russia—was contemplating lowering the nuclear threshold. Over time, this could weaken the broad public support for the nuclear mission that is essential to cohesion.

Unsurprisingly, the communiqué from the July 2016 NATO Summit in Warsaw (which took place after the research phase of this study) devoted significantly more attention to nuclear deterrence issues than its recent predecessors. In it, allied leaders highlighted the fundamental purpose of nuclear weapons—"to preserve peace, prevent coercion, and deter aggression"—and warned that NATO is prepared and able to impose costs on an adversary if the fundamental security of an ally were threatened.[6] This warning in the direction of Moscow—that nuclear use or coercion would be unacceptably risky—is the most explicit the alliance has been since 1999 and reverses a post–Cold War trend toward more ambiguous discussion of NATO's nuclear component. It likewise

---

5. Jeffrey Rathke and Simond Galbert, "NATO's Nuclear Policy as Part of a Revitalized Deterrence Strategy," Center for Strategic and International Studies, January 2016, https://www.csis.org/analysis/nato%E2%80%99s-nuclear-policy-part -revitalized-deterrence-strategy.

6. NATO, "Warsaw Summit Communiqué."

demonstrates a remarkable level of cohesion around the fact that NATO will not be intimidated by nuclear threats and bolsters NATO's overall deterrence policy based on "an appropriate mix of nuclear, conventional, and missile defense capabilities."[7]

All interlocutors agreed that peace and stability in Europe could hinge on Russia's policies and actions. While the alliance's deterrence measures seek to influence Russia's risk calculation, encourage responsible behavior and restraint, and thus render conflict less likely, this cannot be guaranteed. A key question going forward will be whether Russia is prepared to engage in constructive dialogue on nuclear issues and strategic stability.

7. Ibid.

06

Future Challenges to Transatlantic Cohesion

Cohesion is the bedrock on which the transatlantic alliance rests and also its greatest strength; this is a foundational principle but can easily be taken for granted. Does cohesion produce a unified response that is greater than the sum of its parts, or is it achieved only at the lowest common denominator? There are recent examples of both: All 28 allies are contributing to NATO's assurance and deterrence efforts and to the global coalition to counter the Islamic State of Iraq and the Levant (ISIL), signaling unity and resolve in meeting challenges to both the east and south. However, specific contributions to each effort vary dramatically among nations, and differing priorities and threat perceptions have moderated the alliance's level of ambition with regard to both missions.[1] Allies in the east are predictability more focused on the Russia challenge and, as discussed in Section 3, there remains lingering resentment among those we spoke with regarding certain alliance decisions that they view as overly restrained or cautious (e.g., NRFA and VJTF). Allies more focused on southern threats have likewise signaled displeasure about the tepid NATO response to the threat of terrorism, foreign fighters, the strategic implications of the civil war in Syria, the flow of migrants, and the fragile stability of key partners in the region.

The challenges to transatlantic cohesion in responding to modern threats are both internal and external. Internally, challenges to cohesion have political and economic roots. Decades of under-investment in defense by many European allies has caused defense capabilities to atrophy and sowed divisions among allies. Robert Gates, the then U.S. secretary of defense, addressed the growing divide at his final Defense Ministerial in 2011:

> In the past, I've worried openly about NATO turning into a two-tiered alliance: Between members who specialize in "soft' humanitarian, development, peacekeeping, and talking tasks, and those conducting the "hard" combat

---

1. Barack Obama, "Remarks by President Obama in Address to the People of Europe," White House, Office of the Press Secretary (speech, Hannover, Germany, April 25, 2016), https://www.whitehouse.gov/the-press-office/2016/04/25 /remarks-president-obama-address-people-europe; NATO, "NATO's Readiness Action Plan," fact sheet, July 2016, http://www.nato.int/nato_static_fl2014/assets/pdf/pdf_2016_07/20160627_1607-factsheet-rap-en.pdf.

missions. Between those willing and able to pay the price and bear the burdens of alliance commitments, and those who enjoy the benefits of NATO membership—be they security guarantees or headquarters billets—but don't want to share the risks and the costs. This is no longer a hypothetical worry. We are there today. And it is unacceptable.[2]

War fatigue from the enduring operations in Afghanistan and Iraq is another factor impacting cohesion as public support for and confidence in military interventions has decreased more broadly. Additionally, years of uneven economic growth in Europe have gone hand-in-glove with a populist turn in politics that often has illiberal streaks, indicating an internal vulnerability in the values that have traditionally formed the basis of transatlantic unity and cooperation.

Externally, Russian asymmetric activities throughout Europe, as well as the threat of conventional and nuclear warfare, bind all members of the transatlantic alliance. However, as mentioned, national assessments of the principal threat differ. The Baltic States and Poland have pivoted toward a more active role in deterring Russian cross-border aggression, including hosting military exercises and multinational forces, with help from framework nations (the United States, the United Kingdom, Canada, and Germany) and others contributing to a persistent force presence. Meanwhile, nations such as Italy, Turkey, and France have tended to place more focus more on the challenges to NATO's south. Participants emphasized that allies cannot solely focus on narrow security interests but must seek opportunities to contribute across the spectrum of the security response. Examples of measures suggested by our interlocutors included the Baltic States and Poland contributing naval vessels to address the flow of migrants in the Mediterranean, as well as providing logistical and training support for the counter-ISIL coalition. They also thought it should be a priority that countries on the southern flank participate in the multinational forces that form the enhanced deterrence presence in the east.

Moreover, the external threats facing Europe, such as migration and terrorism, do not conform to the boundaries of transatlantic and European institutions: the security of the EU's external border and the functioning of its Schengen Zone depend on intense cooperation with non-EU-member Turkey, while an effective NATO posture in the east and north requires stronger defense engagement and planning with non-NATO partners Finland and Sweden. While NATO and the EU have made progress in practical cooperation in recent years, the issues preventing stronger formal institutional ties remain and may not be resolved quickly. Thus, at the European level, there is an ongoing problem of coordination between a principally civilian institution (the EU) and a primarily military one (NATO), which mirrors in some ways the problems national governments face in civil-military cooperation and between the government and the private sector, for example, on cyber defense. The reliance of eastern flank countries on NATO and the U.S. military for security leaves a gap with the civilian and civilian-military security tasks that NATO is less well positioned to address. Popular skepticism about the EU, which in some cases is abetted by national governments, further weakens the ability of the EU to play its full and essential role in security.

---

2. Robert M. Gates, "Remarks by Secretary Gates at the Security and Defense Agenda," U.S. Department of Defense (speech, Brussels, Belgium, June 10, 2011), http://archive.defense.gov/Transcripts/Transcript.aspx?TranscriptID=4839.

Interlocutors from the Baltic States and Poland were also concerned by the perception that the United States, which has long acted as a balancing force in European politics, has retreated from its traditional leading role in forging common transatlantic approaches to diverse political and security challenges. This is connected in part to a sense that prevailed before 2014 that the most important European issues for the United States had been resolved by post–Cold War reforms in the former socialist countries; by the enlargement of NATO and the EU; and by the deepening integration within the EU. For its part, EU members have in recent years sent fewer demand signals for an activist Washington stance on Europe's internal challenges.

At the same time, burden sharing, a perennial irritant to the U.S.-European relationship, has been too slow to improve. This is no longer a topic of interest only for the circle of Washington Transatlanticists. It has become a central part of the national political debate in the 2016 U.S. presidential election. If progress on burden sharing remains marginal, the readiness of the U.S. Congress and the broader public to devote resources and make sacrifices for transatlantic security will be impacted.

Since the Russian intervention in Ukraine, the tide has begun to turn on the financial aspects of burden sharing within NATO. Allies agreed at the 2014 Wales Summit to "aim to move toward" the spending target of 2 percent of GDP, although the commitment was over a 10-year period and, in light of the economic uncertainty in the euro zone, it was conditioned on continued economic growth.[3] While only five allies meet the target now, two of those are on the eastern flank (Poland and Estonia), and at least 20 of 28 allies increased defense spending in real terms in 2016.[4] As noted previously, Lithuania and Latvia both have been increasing spending rapidly and are committed to reaching the 2 percent level by 2018. These commitments have not been sufficient, however, to reverse a growing public sense in the United States that European allies are "free riders."

Cohesion is to a certain degree a learned behavior that must constantly be relearned. It is a result of common strategic interests and of having institutions and forms of cooperation that are attuned to the challenges of the current day or those that may emerge. Our study revealed a strong degree of cohesion between the Baltic States and Poland on the core issues of their security. We likewise found a high degree of alignment between government officials and the members of civil society we spoke with regarding the desired responses and support from the United States and NATO, along with a deep public awareness of the conventional and nuclear threats facing the region. In keeping with both the internal assessments of their governments and the external demands of their populations, the Baltic States and Poland are making positive strides in devoting significant national resources to strengthening their defenses and to sustaining NATO's focus on the eastern flank. While there were some divergences among them regarding specifics, it was clear from our interactions across the region that there is more that unites these nations than divides them.

---

3. NATO, "Wales Summit Declaration," press release, September 5, 2014, http://www.nato.int/cps/en/natohq/official _texts_112964.htm.

4. Jens Stoltenberg, "Pre-Ministerial Press Conference," NATO (meeting of the North Atlantic Council Defense Ministers, Brussels, Belgium, June 13, 2016), http://www.nato.int/cps/en/natohq/opinions_132272.htm?selectedLocale=en.

About the Project Directors and Authors

Kathleen H. Hicks is senior vice president, Henry A. Kissinger Chair, and director of the International Security Program at CSIS. She is a frequent writer and lecturer on U.S. foreign and security policy; defense strategy, forces, and budget; and strategic futures. Hicks previously served as the principal deputy undersecretary of defense for policy and as deputy undersecretary of defense for strategy, plans, and forces. She led the development of the 2012 Defense Strategic Guidance and the 2010 Quadrennial Defense Review. From 2006 to early 2009, Hicks served as a senior fellow at CSIS, leading a variety of research projects in the national security field. From 1993 to 2006, she was a career civil servant in the Office of the Secretary of Defense, serving in a variety of capacities and rising from Presidential Management Intern to the Senior Executive Service. She holds a PhD in political science from the Massachusetts Institute of Technology, an MA from the University of Maryland's School of Public Affairs, and an AB magna cum laude and Phi Beta Kappa from Mount Holyoke College. Hicks is an adjunct with the RAND Corporation and a member of the Council on Foreign Relations. She served on the National Commission on the Future of the Army and currently serves on the Board of Advisors for the Truman National Security Project and the Board of Advisors for SoldierStrong, a veterans' charity.

Heather A. Conley is senior vice president for Europe, Eurasia, and the Arctic and director of the Europe Program at CSIS. Before joining CSIS in 2009, she served as executive director of the Office of the Chairman of the Board at the American National Red Cross. From 2001 to 2005, she served as deputy assistant secretary of state in the Bureau for European and Eurasian Affairs, with responsibilities for U.S. bilateral relations with the countries of northern and central Europe. From 1994 to 2001, she was a senior associate with an international consulting firm led by former U.S. deputy secretary of state Richard L. Armitage. Conley began her career in the Bureau of Political-Military Affairs at the U.S. Department of State. She was selected to serve as special assistant to the coordinator of U.S. assistance to the newly independent states of the former Soviet Union. Conley is a member of the World Economic Forum's Global Agenda Council on the Arctic and is frequently featured as a foreign policy analyst on CNN, MSNBC, BBC, NPR, and PBS. She received her

BA in international studies from West Virginia Wesleyan College and her MA in international relations from the Johns Hopkins University School of Advanced International Studies.

Lisa Sawyer Samp is a senior fellow in the International Security Program at CSIS, where she focuses on defense strategy and European security. Before joining CSIS, Samp served on the National Security Council staff as director for NATO and European strategic affairs, where she coordinated U.S. policy in preparation for the NATO Summit in Wales and managed the development of plans and force posture assessments to bolster alliance readiness and reassure allies following Russia's aggressive actions in Ukraine. Before her time at the White House, she worked as chief of staff to the assistant secretary of defense for international security affairs, advising on a range of issues related to U.S. defense policy in the Middle East, Europe, Russia/Ukraine/Eurasia, Africa, and the Western Hemisphere. While at the Pentagon, she also held the positions of NATO policy adviser and director for North Africa in the Office of the Secretary of Defense, supporting the full range of defense policy activities related to the 2011 military intervention in Libya. Samp joined the Department of Defense as a Presidential Management Fellow, serving at International Security Assistance Force (ISAF) headquarters in Kabul and at NATO headquarters in Brussels, among other assignments. She is a magna cum laude and Phi Beta Kappa graduate of Baylor University with a BA in international studies and holds an MA in international affairs and development from George Washington University.

Jeffrey Rathke is a senior fellow and deputy director of the Europe Program at CSIS. Previously, he served as the director of the State Department Press Office from May 2014 to June 2015 (and acting deputy spokesperson in April and May 2015). He joined the Foreign Service in 1991 and retired in June 2015. During his Foreign Service tenure, Rathke served as deputy director of the Private Office of the NATO Secretary General in Brussels (2009–2011) and as minister-counselor for political affairs (2006–2009) at the U.S. embassy in Berlin. His Washington assignments included deputy director of the Office of European Security and Political Affairs (EUR/RPM) and duty officer in the White House Situation Room and the State Department Operations Center. Rathke was a Weinberg Fellow at Princeton University from 2003 to 2004, winning the Master's in Public Policy Prize. He served at the U.S. embassy in Dublin from 2001 to 2003, covering multilateral politics during Ireland's tenure on the UN Security Council. From 1999 to 2001, he was posted in Moscow and was responsible for relations with the Russian legislative branch in the Political Section. He was assigned to the U.S. embassy office in Berlin from 1994 to 1996 and helped open the U.S. embassy in Riga from 1992 to 1994. He has been awarded several Superior Honor and Meritorious Honor Awards. Rathke holds an MPP from Princeton University and BA and BS degrees from Cornell University.

Anthony Bell is a research associate with the International Security Program at CSIS, where he works on a range of U.S. defense and security policy issues related to Europe and the Middle East. Before joining CSIS, he worked with the Office of the Secretary of Defense on counterterrorism and security issues in Libya and North Africa. He previously worked as a research assistant at the Institute for the Study of War, focusing on political and security dynamics in Iraq, Afghanistan, and Libya. Since 2013, he has served as an instructional assistant at George Washington University for courses on foreign policy decisionmaking and international security politics. Bell graduated magna cum laude and Phi Beta Kappa from George Washington University with a BA in international affairs and received his MA in security studies from Georgetown University.

www.ingramcontent.com/pod-product-compliance
Lightning Source LLC
Chambersburg PA
CBHW081437270326
41932CB00019B/3243